Look well to this day

Beating Bowel Cancer Mission Statement

Beating Bowel Cancer is a leading UK charity for bowel cancer patients, working to raise awareness of symptoms, promote early diagnosis and encourage open access to treatment choice for those affected by bowel cancer. Through our work we aim to save lives from this common cancer.

Alison Michell

Look well to this day

For Joyce

With best wishes

Alison

Bookmark Publications

January 2013

First published in 2012 by:
Bookmark Publications
61 Sunderland Road
London SE23 2PS

bookmark@pbmail.co.uk

ISBN: 978-0-9560731-1-2

Cover Photograph: Camel Estuary © Alison Michell 2011

Printed and bound in Great Britain by:
Proprint, Remus House, Coltsfoot Drive, Woodston,
Peterborough, PE2 9BF

For my family and friends

Look well to this day
for it is life
the very best of life.
In its brief course lie all
the realities and truth of existence.

For yesterday is but a memory
and tomorrow is only a vision
but today, if well lived, makes
every yesterday a memory of happiness
and every tomorrow a vision of hope.

Look well, therefore, to this day.

(from Sanskrit poem: Salute to the Sun)

ACKNOWLEDGEMENTS

are due to the editors of the following publications in which some of these poems, or versions of them, have previously appeared:

Wavelengths, Waves, The New Writer, One Life Six Words (SMITH Magazine).

Special thanks to Mick Sands at St Christopher's Hospice, London, for his help with the musical settings for the poem 'Look well to this day'; his instrumental accompaniment for solo voice and his choral arrangement have given wings to the author's original melody.

IN MEMORIAM

Mike, Peter, Natalya, Brenda, Beverley and Jen

Look well to this day

Poems

In praise of ordinariness

A day with no appointments, free
from needles and drips, no pain
to speak of. A day to enjoy
soup and sofa and solitude.
Time to relish small tasks, fresh
laundered sheets, casserole
bubbling in the oven, a letter
written, stamped and posted. I work
through my list of chores with pleasure
in the tidy drawer, bills paid, papers
filed. The tradescantia revives
at the taste of water. I wander
from room to room, breathing in
the ordinary, the extraordinary.

On being employed

I didn't seek this. Head hunters
tracked me, trapped me into a contract
for life. I'd willingly surrender
tenure but there's no union to protect
my rights. The job's hard at first,
no training provided. You learn as you go.
Routine becomes drudgery as cycle repeats
cycle with no hope of promotion –
model workers like me earn a sabbatical:
you deserve a break, enjoy the sun,
get away, watch the sand trickle
through the hourglass. When it runs out
my familiar desk is waiting, papers
piled high. One day they'll tell me
they have to let me go. As good employers
they should offer compensation.

Butterfingers

I used to fret in supermarket queue
until I found my fingers turned to thumbs.
It seems I may have met my Waterloo.

Can't fasten buttons, so I say *adieu*
to shirts and jackets, much too bothersome
when hurrying to beat the morning queue.

I drop the cornflakes. Cleaner for the loo
spills on the floor, the checkout girl looks glum
and wishes I had shopped at Waterloo.

I search my purse for money that is due
with digits unaccountably gone dumb,
while others sigh behind me in the queue.

The car key falls, I can't do up my shoe
whose laces have their own curriculum.
I'm going to miss my train at Waterloo.

Incompetence is one of my taboos.
I want to call a moratorium
on being the dud in supermarket queues –
Napoleon disarmed at Waterloo.

Cicatrice

A languorous twelve inch trail
plots the contours of chest wall
from left to right, climbing to a gable
at the sternum, long slow shallow
like the rooftop of a pagoda. Pale
ache in damp weather, its pull
a reminder of the magician who fails
to saw the lady in half. I feel
the bite of metal, hear people
applaud who would be bored by tales
of hospital, surgeon or scalpel.

Appearances

Under my ill-fitting jeans
are crossroads – north south, west east –
moonlit lanes full of potholes.
Only the scanner's eye can tell
what misbehaves. Neuropathy
stings my fingers – you cannot see
the hundred hornets beneath the skin.
Feet are silent stones, lips frozen
by the cold. They manage a wry smile
when people say *You look so well.*

Changing places

Your turn to feel cold gel, metallic slither
of probe into passages once kept for lovers.
I wield the scalpel, masked and gowned,
craft in my fingers, blood on my hands.

Safe and dry in the ops room, I survey
the contours of rocks under a grey sea.
Prisoner in the scanner submarine, you dodge
mines, flinch at the clang of depth charges.

You struggle to breathe, fixed
to hospital plumbing, bleeping, stitched.
I breeze in to flip a chart, feel
a pulse, tell you you're doing well.

I'm the wizard signing prescriptions
for magic potions. Your dried spaghetti veins
taste poison, send it oozing from pores
as you ride the waves in a green reclining chair.

My hand on your arm, mine the compassion
you circle on tiptoe, portal to remission.
Want to know, don't, good news or bad:
your turn to pick the magic card.

Radio Frequency Ablation

Hot clinical rocket
homes in on target –

bulls eye – tumour
cannot escape pursuer.

Tissue is burning
up, smelting

in the body's crucible.
Rebellious cells

cured like Arbroath smokies.
I am done to a turn. Lucky.

Hangover – 4 am

Thinning hair, peeling thumbs,
raging thirst, rebellious tum,
legs are wobbly, toes are numb,
tired and weary, sleep won't come.
It wasn't vodka, gin or rum –
chemotherapy damage done.

Woodcraft

For months it passed unnoticed in a thicket.
Long-limbed birch with branches
a boy might swing on. Resilient against drought

with a small thirst quenched
by moisture from the nearby beck,
rustling its leaves with beech and larch

in neighbourly gossip till a rough patch of bark
attracts a passing woodpecker
hungry for grubs. His diamond beak

rat-a-tats machine gun fire through silver
fuselage, hammer blows dead on target
to uncover not food but the canker

beneath, early warning of the blight
which takes so many trees across the valley.
Deep under the leaf mould, taproot

braces trunk to hold steady
against the bite of pruning shears
while leaves with no visible sign of decay
wilt in the forester's toxic sprays.

Reprieve

A stay of execution's not to be confused
with a pardon. I'll not confess
my guilt, hope for release

but they lock me back in my cell. I wonder
how long this time. It might be easier
if I'd committed murder

or sold state secrets, but my mistakes
do not add up unless you take
account of Saturday bacon

sandwiches I should have refused. Guards
reward cooperation – an extra period
of rest – but clemency's denied.

We have exhausted every avenue. Innocence
in the end seems to make no difference.
I'd give my life for a life sentence.

Liver

When a Frenchman feels off colour he'll blame
a *crise de foie*, sipping his *tisane* to relieve
discomfort. A matter for correct translation
since this crisis has nothing to do with faith.
His conscience is clear and no mid-life angst
upsets his equilibrium. His liver
is out of sorts. All he needs is peppermint
or camomile to soothe his troubled digestion.
My English organ is not so easily restored
to health. The body's river system ferries
spores which pollute its marshes. Dredgers
help to clear hepatic channels, sluices
keep the bile streams flowing; poison
seeps through the yellowing sedge.

First things

Before the weighing and measuring,
before blood is siphoned for testing,
before they connect the drip –

the first thing they ask me
when I check in
is what I want for lunch.

No stomach for braised lamb shanks,
and I suspect the oxtail soup
would be a mistake.

I could fancy a ginger biscuit
served with Darjeeling
or consommé and wafer-thin toast.

Mirror, mirror on the wall

Builders have removed my mirror
taken down the bathroom wall.
As my skin is now in tatters
this is surely just as well.

No more searching for perfection,
I'm no longer fair of face.
I've lost sight of my reflection,
Alice has no looking glass.

Blemish, blotches, spot and pimple,
drugs have put them all on show.
Underneath it's one big gamble
will it make the cancer go?

Bring me pots of aloe vera
lavender and calamine.
Coat my lashes with mascara,
soften lips with vaseline.

Ointments, creams and healing lotions
try to soothe my damaged pores.
Give me back my old complexion
make me better, find a cure.

Because we're worth it

Your skin a smooth scalpel skim,
eyebrows raised by the puppeteer.
No hint of wattle under that sculpted
Hepburn chin but I see your mottled hands
sneak into the sanctuary of pockets. No crows
have tiptoed round your eyes. I wonder
how often you smile now, if your forehead
allows a frown at my excesses as it did
when we were young. That size 8 straitjacket,
prize for abstention, suffocates the girl
I knew whose favourite was trifle. Wake up,
join my campaign against Botox, share the joke
as we trip sprightly in purple. Let's laugh
at misfortune and rejoice in our wrinkles.

Six words

Lost my hair, kept my cool.

Look good, feel better

If you wear the right
mascara, they say you can
cut your stress in half

Abutilon

One fierce winter is enough to cause concern
about survival. Even in a sheltered spot the abutilon
struggles, being only half hardy. But with spring

comes remission of a sort – developing buds uneven,
fewer in number, vine-shaped leaves stripped of sheen,
Orange Bell less sprightly in her dance.

A second year of unprecedented freeze
brings arctic wind, snow on snow, frost
knuckling into ailing roots – we fear the worst.

The thaw reveals wizened branches we can snap
with our bare hands down to the brittle stump.
No hint of growth, no shoots, any lingering sap

dormant. We look in vain for signs of foliage,
the light sending hints and shimmers, mirage
to tantalise. The day we fetch the spade, a smudge

of palest green, flicker of colour. And she grows –
hardy after all – slimmer now with a glamorous
viridian trim round each apricot lantern globe.

Sundial

Stone honed
by wind and rain
pale as old bone.
No sound.
Every day
all day
bound by shaft
of light and heat
– neither early
nor late –
mark each silent beat
never repeat
a minute
tell it straight.

A good year

Free to travel with my bus pass,
cheaper tickets at the play.
No more charges for prescriptions –
I turned sixty yesterday.

Hope I'll manage on my pension,
smaller bills, less tax to pay.
Gordon helps me with the gas bills –
I turned sixty yesterday.

Let's not talk about the wrinkles
or the fact my hair's turned grey
since it means that purple suits me –
I turned sixty yesterday.

I've gone back to being a student.
Workshops, essays come my way
though I'm older than my tutors –
I turned sixty yesterday.

Stallone, Lumley, Cher and Clinton,
nineteen forty six holds sway.
Here's to vintage baby boomers –
I turned sixty yesterday.

For want of a nail

Fishmonger and butcher
discontinued, bank and post office
long gone. Corner bakery
turned into tanning parlour
last year and even the off licence
has run dry. Where are dry cleaner
and shoe mender? Nobody remembers
greengrocer or florist. But tucked away
in a thicket of To Let signs you'll find
the hardware store
which holds my life together: hinges
to open my doors, oil to stop them creaking.
There is filler for my cracks, pointing
for the brickwork, putty to seal my sashes
against the rain. Different grades of sandpaper
smooth rough edges, varnish preserves
the finished grain. This is my shop, stocking
tin tacks and fuses, bath plugs and lagging
for the pipes. My kingdom of small things.

How is it for you . . . ?

standing forlorn as they wheel me off on a trolley

counting tubes, trying not to look at drains

cursing the car park ticket machine – out of change again

wondering why I don't remember your two visits yesterday

crying because I forgot yesterday was your birthday

cross-examining the consultant, if you can find him

worrying if I'll manage the stairs when I get home

cooking my favourite dish which no longer tempts me

running out of patience with my twinges

wishing I'd do my share of the washing up

pretending to sleep through my waking nightmares

longing for someone to ask how *you* are

feeling guilty when you want a day at the shops

holding my hand as we wait for the scan

talking to me though you can't be sure I hear

looking back, looking forward, carrying on

After the tone

When I ring, usual time, your voice
says *leave a message.* Presence
of an absence.

If you're in the garden, my news
can wait. Clip of secateurs
dead-heading roses.

I'll tell you another day of lilies
illuminating our sadness,
how you were missed.

I call again, again, again. Listen
to silence, learn the absence
of your presence.

Odds

Cancer strikes at one
in three: now when we meet you
two are off the hook

Act of faith

My passport is due for renewal.
Will that make me viable
for another ten years?
The photo shows cropped hair
above an optimistic smile, exposes
flecks of anxiety in the eyes.

Time

Some days we waste time –
as if we could recycle
those unused minutes

In the valley of the shadow

A place where shade and light
take turns, not equal but with more
sun than I expected. There are trees
for shelter and a willow leaning
over the stream to dip its leaves
where the water flows deep.
I have put stepping stones across
the widest part, joining a grassy bank
on one side with that rocky overhang
opposite. Dark clouds in the offing
make the bright patches of blue
bluer. A meadow stretches
up the hill, speckled with wild orchids
in spring, poppies in summer. I walk
here often, nobody in sight to disturb
my thoughts, find my fears calmed
by the spirit which inhabits this place.

On parade

Mustered at the bottom of the wardrobe
in dusty reproach to polished standards
he kept though fingers fumbled over laces –
brown brogues beside plain black size twelves
worn with fine silk socks and City bowler.

I place my smaller feet in the vast spaces,
remember how he stumbled over kerbs,
tripped behind the Zimmer – then the shift
to a soft-shoe shuffle, slippers
dyed the colour of his favourite claret.

He would not let them go unbrushed,
without their wooden stretchers: line them up,
give a last coat of Cherry Blossom
before dismissing them to Oxfam shelves.

Leftovers

At the back of the fridge
there is always a pot
of forgotten mince, a cold potato
in a blue-striped bowl.

Whiskery lemons jostle for space
with half an apple wrapped in cling film,
and a flotilla of small jugs,
each with its skim of milk.

Her shopping remembers
his appetite for pies,
small print on the packets,
the calories he should have counted.

She drinks tea, pecks at biscuit crumbs,
no longer troubled by hunger.

Marmalade

The Alhambra's sun
warming my winter kitchen.
Oranges on a scrubbed table.

The old preserving pan
down from the attic.
My mother's sticky recipe.

She snipped the peel
to matchstick shreds
with scissors.

A wooden spoon.
My arm aching
as hers did.

Her voice reminds me
to keep the pips
for their pectin

and chill saucers
in the fridge
to test for a set.

A cauldron surging.
The tawny gloss
of a rolling boil.

Tang of citrus
stings the air, stain
of its oil on my fingers.

Sweet bite on my tongue
recaptures the morning rush
to catch the school bus.

I'll store the jars on larder shelves.
Amber jelly holding
shadows from Granada.

Daughter

My left shoe props open the door
to the landing. I wake the instant
before I hear your shuffle, as instinct
once alerted me to a change
in my baby's breathing. It's not hunger
which gets you up. I listen
for the flush, for the pad
of your slippers, count your steps.
Wait till I hear a quiet snore
as you drift back into sleep
without the lullaby
I hum to settle myself.

The party frock

Your memory's a pigeon homing back
to the house where you were born, creak
on the top stair, green swings in the park.

You're smart in khaki at the wheel
of a three-ton lorry, or driving a general
to his rendezvous. You still turn pale

remembering the telegram with news
of a brother. *Regret, missing, presumed.* Choose
not to hear *dead.* These things stay as you lose

your grip on yesterday. You fail to count back
from a hundred, puzzled by this trick
question which tells them nothing of the frock

you made for my tenth birthday, measured
by your seamstress' eye, sleeves embroidered
with blue and silver moons which shimmered

in orbit round my arms. Your broad sewing thumb,
bleached with French chalk, sets the width of a seam.
Watch me show off my sash and the swirl of the hem.

Mind games

In the kitchen you hopscotch
with ingredients, juggle recipes -
this year the marmalade won't set.
Grandmother's footsteps sneak to the car,
safety lecture falling on deaf ears
so we play hide and seek with keys. I hate
these games, the way wily memories
shadow-box, sidestepping out of reach.

Except that the holiday in Brodick 1934
is Box Brownie sharp. You climb Goat Fell,
beat your favourite brother three and two
skipping all the bunkers. Still on the course
approaching ninety, a bit the worse
for wear with pacemaker and low
blood pressure, let me be your ball
of string to keep the way secure.

Walk in my shoes

If I were to walk in your shoes, I'd know
what it is to grow old. Flash and flicker
of memory, everybody talking
too fast and not loud enough. I would hate
my walking stick, signs of independence
dwindling as cooking skills and then my car
fall into disuse. Would I celebrate
each new birthday when enough seems enough?

Put your feet in mine and you'd understand
that growing old is what I long to do.
You'd swap my bad prognosis for stiff knees,
my pills for yours, my hospital routine
for all your extra years. Scans and needles
would become a bore. Perhaps you'd hanker
after grandchildren, for ninety candles
on your cake and tranquil days unwinding?

Snowbound

I sigh over missed appointments. You clap hands
at another day off school. I predict shortages
in the store cupboard. You say we'll bake
cakes if the bread runs out. I try not to worry
about heating bills. You dance joyously
round your first snowman. I fret
over frozen pipes. You catch snowflakes
on your tongue. I lament my failure
to invest in chains. You ransack the attic
for the sledge. Cold feet forgotten, we hurtle
downhill. I show you how to turn yourself
into a snow angel. We scatter our crusts
for the hungry birds. I'm starting to see things
your way, dodge a snowball, throw one back.

Pattern

This time my own design –
longer-lasting yarns
to match sea-washed pebbles,
cables twisting their dance
above ladders of ribbing.
Tension will be loose.
No need for buttons
or tight cuffs. Spread wide
raglan sleeves – cast off.

Jitterbug

Your face says it. We're back
at the bottom of the snake.

There's talk of a trial,
surely a worthwhile

use of funding. A regime
in the diary. I'm calm

under fire. When the news
is good I get the jitters.

How to manage on parole
without comfortable rules?

I jump at shadows, step over
cracks in the pavement. Danger

has a fringe of luck,
freedom's edged in black.

Under the wire

No tunnel this time, all that earth
to disperse. I opt for disguise,
forged papers, much rehearsal
of how to answer a challenge:
*Whatever you do, don't reply
in English.* The absence
of moon is a stroke of luck
though it makes it harder
to find the track. The map
meticulously traced on a scrap
torn from a hymnbook
isn't much help. Once word
gets out, I'll be a marked man
a long way from home.

Terminus

Somewhere down the track points
have shifted, clearing the train
to head towards its destination.
No one has calculated when
it will get here: the laws of mechanics
teach us that time equals distance
over speed, so we need to know
how far off it is, how fast it will go.

Marathon

You wouldn't take me for an athlete —
No real turn of speed and my feet
are flat.

I never sprint for trains or buses,
my only team success
lacrosse.

Faced with this unwelcome marathon
I am a reluctant Olympian.
I run

sedate and stubborn, a slow back of the pack
jogger looking for a breather, a drink
in bleak

dank streets beside the river. Overtaken
by those who trained, each one keen
to win

a medal, you'll not find me on the podium.
I want to be last into the stadium —
anthem

plays for others. Give me the wooden spoon,
a booby prize, penny for the ferryman.
Race done.

There is no Stage Five . . .

or so they say, as if to rub it in, when grave voices
give their prognosis. They sound certain, but who knows
if we are born only once? I might come back
as a leopardess, or a marquise in a velvet cloak.

I could be a silver birch, maybe an undiscovered moon
beyond this galaxy. I'd like you to imagine
me somewhere, intangible. Tune in carefully,
you might be able to pick up my signal.

Be careful what you wish for

A chemo diet keeps hunger quiet –
not so much food to chew.
My teenage dreams of size 10 jeans
have finally come true.

My straight bob went and baldness meant
a cold and stubbly head.
Then curls I longed for as a girl
bloomed like flowers instead.

So when I'm told *Do not grow old*
my answer's loud and clear:
that still there's scope for me to hope
for just another year.

Endgame

They say that hearing is the last to fade,
that ears are finely tuned to whispered sounds.
Come talk to me, let silence be delayed.

When taste has gone and sight has been betrayed
by dark, familiar voices gather round.
They say that hearing is the last to fade.

Touch lingers too. I feel a warm hand laid
on mine, but words provide a richer ground.
Come sing for me, let silence be delayed

by songs, melody and counterpoint played
softly, chords and cadences interwound.
They say that hearing is the last to fade.

Tell tales and gossip, do not be dismayed
at no response. My laughter is housebound.
Come joke with me, let silence be delayed.

I'm listening, my terrors far outweighed
by syllables whose comfort is profound.
They say that hearing is the last to fade,
Come talk, joke, sing – and silence is delayed.

Look well to this day

In quiet interludes we say – look well to this day
In troubled times let's pray – look well to this day
Whatever fortune comes your way – look well to this day
Look well to this day, look well to this day.

When sick or frightened don't dismay – look well to this day
When everything looks grey – look well to this day
When faced with illness and decay – look well to this day
Look well to this day, look well to this day.

Don't dwell on pains of yesterday – look well to this day
Tomorrow's far away – look well to this day
Live every moment, come what may – look well to this day
Look well to this day, look well to this day.

This poem has been set to music for solo voice and choir. For further details or to obtain a copy, please contact Bookmark Publications